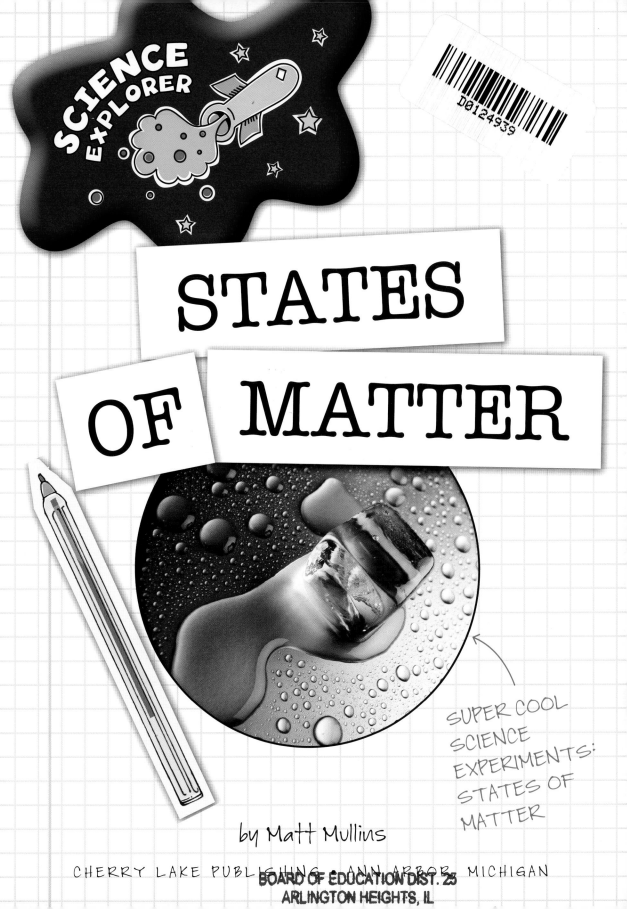

SCIENCE EXPLORER

STATES OF MATTER

SUPER COOL
SCIENCE
EXPERIMENTS:
STATES OF
MATTER

by Matt Mullins

CHERRY LAKE PUBLISHING · ANN ARBOR, MICHIGAN

A NOTE TO PARENTS AND TEACHERS: Please review the instructions for these experiments before your children do them. Be sure to help them with any experiments you do not think they can safely conduct on their own.

A NOTE TO KIDS: Be sure to ask an adult for help with these experiments when you need it. Always put your safety first!

CHERRY LAKE
Publishing

Published in the United States of America by
Cherry Lake Publishing
Ann Arbor, Michigan
www.cherrylakepublishing.com

Content Editor: Robert Wolffe, EdD,
Professor of Teacher Education,
Bradley University, Peoria, Illinois

Book design and illustration: The Design Lab

Photo Credits: Cover and page 1, ©Janpietruszka/Dreamstime.com; page 4, Laurence Gough, used under license from Shutterstock, Inc.; page 7, ©Carolinasmith/Dreamstime.com; page 15, ©Kamchatka/Dreamstime.com; page 16, ©iStockphoto.com/RonBailey; page 19, ©iStockphoto.com/RGebbiePhoto; page 20, ©iStockphoto.com/WitR; page 24, ©Anthony Harris, used under license from Shutterstock, Inc.; page 28, ©Skazka/Dreamstime.com

Library of Congress Cataloging-in-Publication Data
Mullins, Matt.
   Super cool science experiments: States of matter / by Matt Mullins.
      p. cm.—(Science explorer)
   Includes bibliographical references and index.
   ISBN-13: 978-1-60279-535-8   ISBN-10: 1-60279-535-5 (lib. bdg.)
   ISBN-13: 978-1-60279-614-0   ISBN-10: 1-60279-614-9 (pbk.)
1. Matter—Constitution—Experiments—Juvenile literature. 2. Matter—Juvenile literature. I. Title. II. Title: States of matter. III. Series.
   QC173.16.M85 2010
   530.4078—dc22   2009011577

Cherry Lake Publishing would like to acknowledge the work of The Partnership for 21st Century Skills. Please visit www.21stcenturyskills.org for more information.

SCIENCE EXPLORER

STATES OF MATTER

TABLE OF CONTENTS

What's the Matter?

Would you like to be a scientist?

Matter is anything that has weight. All natural stuff is matter. The forms that matter takes on are called states. We usually think about three states of matter. We see things around us as solids. These include rock or ice. Another state of matter includes liquids, such as water. There are also gases, such as the air we breathe.

Scientists study matter down to its smallest unit—the atom. They study how atoms bind together in molecules.

In this book, you will learn how to study matter like a physicist or chemist. You will learn how to create your own experiments, too! You don't need a fancy lab to get started. You will see how you can use things you already have at home to investigate matter. By thinking like a scientist, you'll learn a lot of things about matter.

First Things First

Scientists take good notes so they don't forget any details.

Scientists learn about matter by watching and testing it. Good scientists write down their observations. You can do this, too.

When scientists design experiments, they must think very clearly. The way they think about problems is often called the scientific method. What is the scientific method? It's a step-by-step way of finding answers to specific questions. The steps don't always follow the same pattern. Sometimes scientists change their minds. The process often works something like this:

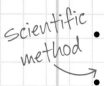
Scientific method

- **Step One:** A scientist gathers the facts and makes observations about one particular thing.
- **Step Two:** The scientist comes up with a question that is not answered by all the observations and facts.
- **Step Three:** The scientist creates a hypothesis. This is a statement of what the scientist thinks is probably the answer to the question.
- **Step Four:** The scientist tests the hypothesis. He or she designs an experiment to see whether the hypothesis is correct. The scientist does the experiment and writes down what happens.
- **Step Five:** The scientist draws a conclusion based on how the experiment turned out. The conclusion might be that the hypothesis is correct. Sometimes, though, the hypothesis is not correct. In that case, the scientist might develop a new hypothesis and another experiment.

By following along with this book, you will use the scientific method in your own home. Your kitchen will become your very own laboratory! You will test hypotheses and come to conclusions. Let's get started, scientists!

Experiment #1
Matter Bonds

You can make models of molecules. This is a model of a water molecule—two hydrogen atoms bonded to one oxygen atom.

Matter is made up of atoms. An atom is the smallest piece of matter that still has the properties of that material or element. One or more atoms of any kind that bond, or stick together, are called molecules. Some molecules are multiple atoms of the same kind. Picture the oxygen molecules in the air we breathe. That oxygen is made up of molecules of two oxygen atoms. You may have seen an oxygen molecule described as O_2. That is a way of describing two oxygen atoms that join to form one molecule of the element oxygen. Other molecules bond atoms to form compounds of different materials. Water is a compound. A water molecule, or H_2O, combines two hydrogen atoms with one oxygen atom.

Molecules bind with other molecules to make up a substance. The force of attraction between molecules is different for different substances. The bond is stronger in some kinds of matter than it is in others.

Let's investigate this. Have you ever noticed that rain often rests on a surface in rounded drops instead of spreading out in a thin film? Scientists know that the hydrogen atoms in a molecule of water are not only attracted to the oxygen atom in that same molecule. They are also attracted to nearby oxygen atoms. Could this mean that water molecules might be more strongly attracted to each other than the molecules of other liquids are? Our hypothesis can be: **Water molecules are attracted to one another more than the molecules of some other liquids are attracted to one another.**

Here's what you'll need:
- 3 small glasses
- Water
- Dish soap
- Plastic spoon
- Dish towel
- Rubbing alcohol
- 2 medicine droppers

How many drops can you add before the liquid spills over?

Notes:

Instructions:

1. Fill 2 glasses ¾ full of water. Add several drops of dish soap to 1 glass. Stir well with the spoon.

2. Add more water up to the rim of both glasses. Use the towel to dry off the sides of the glasses without disturbing the liquid inside.

3. Fill the third glass to the rim with rubbing alcohol. Be very careful when using rubbing alcohol. Do not work near an open flame. Be sure not to get any in your mouth or eyes.

4. Fill 1 of the droppers with water. Drip water into the glass that's filled with plain water. See if you can make the water bulge up in a dome above the rim of the glass. Write down what you observe.

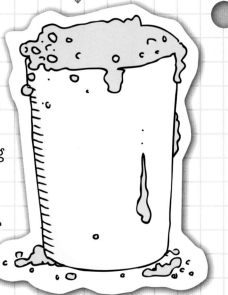

What happens when you use soapy water?

5. Fill the same dropper with soapy water. Drip soapy drops into the glass with soapy water. Can you make the soapy water bulge up by adding enough drops? Record what you see.

6. Fill the other dropper with rubbing alcohol. Add drops to the glass of rubbing alcohol. Can you make that liquid bulge? Write down your observations.

Conclusion:

What happened as you added drops and the liquids reached over the rim of the glasses? Did all of the liquids behave in the same way?

At the surface of many liquids, the molecules are attracted to other molecules next to and below them. The attraction can be strong, forming a thin skin at the surface. This is called surface tension. Surface tension helps the molecules of certain liquids stay together. They form a dome instead of spilling over the glass. Soap weakens surface tension. Also, gravity becomes stronger than the attraction between molecules when you add too many drops. Does this explain your results? Would you conclude that the molecules of certain liquids bonded better than others? Was your hypothesis correct?

Experiment #2
Solids, Liquids, and Gases

A solid is matter in which molecules have less energy and can hold on to one another tightly. The attraction between the molecules keeps them in place. Molecules are always attracted to one another. As they get more energy, however, the ability to move allows them to overcome this pull toward one another. In a liquid, they can move enough to go past one another. But the attraction still keeps them grouped together. In a gas, there is so much energy that the attraction can no longer keep them next to one another. Gas molecules rush around in every direction.

Even though molecules are attracted tightly in a solid, they do vibrate. But you don't see your kitchen table trembling, do you? The molecules in the table are jiggling, though. They're just so small and the movements are so tiny that you can't tell they move. Molecules in liquid also move. Again, you can't see the molecules moving. Even though a liquid's molecules are packed together tightly, they have more space between them than in a solid. They flow around one another and move about. In a gas, molecules move around freely.

As matter warms up, the added energy makes the molecules move more. The molecules in a solid become less tightly packed together. As the energy to move becomes stronger than the forces of attraction, the solid becomes a liquid. In a liquid, what happens to the attraction the molecules have for one another as they gain energy? The molecules let go of one another and go all over the place! Does all this mean we can change states of matter by adding heat? Can we use heat to change the state of water? Develop a hypothesis. Here is one option: **By adding heat, the state of water can be changed from a solid to a liquid to a gas.**

Here's what you'll need:
- Ice cubes
- 1-gallon (3.8 liter) resealable plastic freezer bag
- Microwave oven
- An adult

Take careful notes so you can share your results with other scientists.

Instructions:

1. Place 2 ice cubes in the freezer bag. Lay the bag flat on a counter. Push the bag as flat as you can before sealing it. Now there is very little air in the bag.

2. Place the bag in the microwave. Ask an adult to run the microwave for 20 seconds. Watch through the microwave oven window as the ice heats. Have the adult continue to run the microwave for 20-second periods until the ice has completely melted.

3. Have the adult run the microwave for more 20-second intervals to see if you can change the liquid into a gas. Do you notice a change in the bag? Write down your observations.

Conclusion:

How much time does it take for the ice to melt into a liquid? As you continue to heat it, what happens to the liquid? What happens to the bag? Does the bag stay the same size? Does it expand? Why?

Ice is a solid. The water molecules are attracted to one another and slow down. Heating the ice causes some important changes. The molecules gain energy. They vibrate more. If the molecules gain enough energy, they will not be attracted to one another so strongly. They slide about and past one another. The solid becomes a liquid. Adding more heat to the liquid causes the molecules to move even faster. The molecules eventually gain enough energy to pass beyond the molecules that are at the liquid's surface. These molecules rise up into the air as a gas or water vapor. This process is called evaporation. If your bag expanded, could this vapor be the reason why? Was your hypothesis correct?

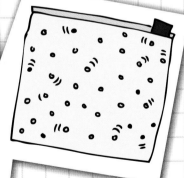

Which bag represents a solid? A liquid? A gas?

Changes in water from ice to liquid to gas are physical changes. The water is still water, whatever its state. It remains H_2O. Sometimes matter changes into something different. When that happens, we call it a chemical change. Burning wood causes a chemical change. Wood is hydrogen and carbon bound together. When wood is burned, the hydrogen and carbon separate. The hydrogen floats away. The ash is the carbon that is left behind. Ash is not wood—it's chemically different.

Have you ever created a chemical change? You have if you've started a campfire!

Experiment #3

Matter Takes Up Space

↰ What happens when you fill a container with too much liquid?

Matter always takes up space. A solid keeps its shape no matter where you place it. A liquid takes the shape of whatever container you put it in. Gas fills up whatever container it is in. Put gas in a balloon, and it will be shaped like a balloon. In a box, it's shaped like a box. Put gas from a small balloon into a big box with a lid, and it will spread out to fill the entire box.

If you had a big bottle of water and tried to pour it all into a little bottle, what would happen? Would the liquid overflow? What if you tried to do the same with a bottle of gas? Scientists know that gas will work with whatever space it has, to a certain limit. We call that available space volume.

Do liquids and gases react differently to changes in the spaces they take up? Think about water and air. Our hypothesis could be: **Water of a certain volume can't be contained in a space with a smaller volume, but air of a certain volume can be contained in a space that has a smaller volume.**

Here's what you'll need:
- 2 identical empty dish soap bottles with caps
- Water
- Air

You don't need many materials for this experiment.

17

Instructions:

1. Fill 1 of the bottles all the way to the top with water. Screw the cap on tightly.
2. Open the other bottle to let air in. Screw the cap on tightly.
3. Squeeze the bottle filled with water. What happens? Can you squeeze it very much? Write down your observations.
4. Hold the water bottle over the sink with the nozzle on top. Open the nozzle. Squeeze the bottle. What did you observe this time?
5. Make sure the nozzle of the bottle filled with air is closed. Hold your finger over the nozzle and squeeze the bottle. Are you able to make it smaller?

Be sure to work over the sink to avoid making a watery mess.

Conclusion:

What did you observe? Could you feel the bottle of water resist, or push against, your hand as you tried to squeeze it with the cap closed? Would the water let you squeeze it into a smaller space? What did the water do when you opened the cap and squeezed? Did creating a space for the water to go allow you to make the space in the bottle smaller? How did the air in the second bottle react to the squeezing? Were you able to squeeze the bottle even though the cap was closed? What does this tell you about the ability of air to be compressed, or squeezed together? There is more space between gas molecules than the molecules of a liquid. Does this help explain your findings? What can you conclude about the behavior of water and air in an equal space?

Can you apply what you learned? How could you get the honey to pour out faster?

Experiment #4
Density and Weight

Which is more dense? The oranges or the 1 kilogram weight?

All matter—solids, liquids, and gases—has weight. All matter also has density. Although they are related, density is not the same as weight. Picture 1 pound (0.45 kilogram) of cotton candy and 1 pound of gold. They both weigh 1 pound. But it would take a small bag to hold the gold and a huge bag to hold the cotton candy. That's because gold is denser than cotton candy. Gold takes up much less space than an equal weight of cotton candy. Think of density as the amount of mass or molecules packed into a certain space. The more you pack into a set amount of space, the denser it is and the more it weighs.

Different types of matter have different densities. We've seen this to be true with two solids: gold and cotton candy. Can the same be true for different liquids? Let's use 3 common liquids: rubbing alcohol, water, and cooking oil. Here are 2 hypotheses that can be tested with the same experiment:

Hypothesis #1: Rubbing alcohol is denser than cooking oil.

Hypothesis #2: Water is denser than rubbing alcohol.

Here's what you'll need:
- Glass jar
- Rubbing alcohol
- Blue and red food coloring
- Plastic spoon
- Funnel with a long tip
- Vegetable oil
- Water
- Drinking glass

Instructions:

1. Fill ¼ of the jar with rubbing alcohol. Add several drops of blue food coloring to the alcohol, and stir with the spoon. You now have a blue liquid.

2. Put the funnel over the mouth of the jar. The tip of the funnel should be long enough to extend down toward the bottom of the jar.

3. Pour in vegetable oil until the jar is another ¼ full of this liquid. Remove the funnel. Which liquid is on top? Which is on the bottom?

4. Put some water in a glass. Add drops of red food coloring to make a red liquid.

5. Pour the red water through the funnel into the jar. Stop when about ¼ of the jar is full of water.

Why do you think we use a funnel in this experiment?

Conclusion:

Observe the liquid layers. Do you see 3 bands of liquid? Which is on top? Which is on the bottom? Which is in the center? The one on the bottom is the densest. The one on the top is the least dense. Is alcohol denser or less dense than cooking oil? Is water more or less dense than alcohol? Is water more or less dense than oil? Did you prove your hypotheses?

Water is weird. It is a special type of matter that is denser as a liquid than it is as a solid. Most stuff is denser as a solid. Melted gold has less density as a liquid than as a solid. Drop solid gold into liquid gold, and it sinks right to the bottom. But add ice to a glass of water and it floats!

Experiment #5
Matter Can Be Supercool

How do you get flavored water to stay on a stick? Freeze it!

The freezing point of a liquid is the temperature at which it turns into a solid. For water, that's 32 degrees Fahrenheit (0 degrees Celsius). When a liquid becomes solid, the attraction between the molecules holds the molecules very close to one another. So the freezing point is the stage at which the bonds between molecules of matter are strong enough to keep all the molecules in place. All they can do is vibrate.

When a liquid gets colder, its molecules need a little energy to lock themselves into place. They have enough energy in their liquid state to do this. But we can affect that. We can use science to supercool a liquid—cool it fast so that, even below its freezing point, it stays liquid!

Scientists know that a supercooled liquid needs a little bit of a jolt, a little extra energy, to suddenly freeze. It's as if the molecules need a reminder to change their grip. They need to be disturbed, or given a "push" to become solid. Could this concept be applied to water? What do you think? Let's try it. Here is one option for a hypothesis: **Water can be supercooled and needs to be disturbed before it can freeze.**

Here's what you'll need:
- 6 bottles of distilled water or high quality spring water
- Refrigerator
- Freezer
- Kitchen towel

Your kitchen will be your lab for this experiment.

Instructions:

1. Chill the water bottles in the refrigerator overnight.
2. Gently remove the bottles from the fridge. Examine them carefully. You only want water that does not have bubbles in it.
3. Choose 3 bottles without bubbles in them. Place them in the freezer carefully, to avoid making any bubbles in the water. They should be set in the freezer in an upright position. For the next 3 hours, make sure no one bumps the freezer or disturbs it in any way.
4. After 3 hours, remove the bottles of water. Gently place them on a countertop. Tip the bottles a bit to make sure they are still liquid. Very gently wipe off the outside of the bottles with the towel if they are clouded with dew.
5. Take a bottle and tap it on the counter. What happens?
6. Repeat the process with the other 2 bottles.

What happens when you give the bottle a tap?

Conclusion:

What happened when you disturbed the water by banging the bottle on a hard surface? Did it freeze? If so, how does this happen? In a properly supercooled bottle of water, the liquid will turn to ice at one spot when you disturb it. The ice will quickly spread. The whole bottle will turn to ice in seconds right before your eyes! Amazing, isn't it?

The science behind supercooling is complicated. Adding energy by disturbing the water and making molecules bump into one another is not the only reason the water freezes. Molecules also need to form as solids around something. That "something" might be an extra-cool spot on the container or a bubble created by shaking. That's why the experiment doesn't work if the water has a bubble in it before supercooling, or if the water isn't very pure. If something extra is in the water, the ice may form around that substance.

Experiment #6
Do It Yourself!

You can cook up some scientific fun in your kitchen!

It's time to continue learning through your own experiments. Start in your kitchen. Try determining the temperature at which liquid water turns to gas. What would your hypothesis be? How would you run an experiment to find the answer? What kitchen tools would you use?

Or you could mix a solid such as salt with a liquid such as water. Could you find a way to get the salt back after mixing it in water? How could your knowledge of the states of matter—and water in particular—help you find a way? What would your experiment be?

You've learned a lot about the states of matter. You've even found a way to make water supercool! Experiments may not always turn out just as you planned. But by thinking like a scientist, you've gained some important tools. They will help you learn more about the world around you. Isn't that what matters?

Can you find three states of matter in this picture?

GLOSSARY

atom (AT-uhm) the smallest part of an element that still has the properties of the element

conclusion (kuhn-KLOO-zhuhn) a final decision, thought, or opinion

evaporation (i-vah-puh-RAY-shuhn) the process in which a liquid changes to a gas or vapor

hypothesis (hy-POTH-uh-sihss) a logical guess about what will happen in an experiment

method (METH-uhd) a way of doing something

molecules (MOL-uh-kyoolz) the smallest forms of a material that have the chemical properties of the material and are made up of two or more atoms

observations (ob-zur-VAY-shuhnz) things that are seen or noticed with one's senses

states (STAYTSS) forms of matter

supercool (soo-pur-KOOL) to lower the temperature of something below its freezing point without it becoming solid

volume (VOL-yuhm) the amount of space taken up by a three-dimensional object or substance

FOR MORE INFORMATION

BOOKS

Claybourne, Anna. *The Science of a Glass of Water: The Science of States of Matter*. Pleasantville, NY: Gareth Stevens Publishing, 2008.

Gardner, Robert. *Melting, Freezing, and Boiling Science Projects with Matter*. Berkeley Heights, NJ: Enslow Elementary, 2006.

Oxlade, Chris. *Solids: An Investigation*. New York: PowerKids Press, 2008.

WEB SITES

BBC—Science: Chemistry: Particles and State Changes

www.bbc.co.uk/schools/ks3bitesize/science/chemistry/physical_changes_6.shtml

Watch what happens to the particles of a substance when it is heated or cooled

BBC—Science: Materials: Gases, Liquids and Solids

www.bbc.co.uk/schools/ks2bitesize/science/activities/gases.shtml

Try this fun activity, and learn more about the states of matter

PBS Kids—ZOOMsci: Floating Paper Clips

pbskids.org/zoom/activities/sci/floatingpaperclips.html

Run another experiment about surface tension

INDEX

About the → Author

Matt Mullins holds a master's degree in the history of science. He lives in Madison, Wisconsin, with his wife and son. Matt writes about science and technology, food and wine, and other topics that interest him.